Been There!
MEXICO

by Annabel Savery

A+

Smart Apple Media

Facts about Mexico

Population: 107 million

Capital City: Mexico City

Currency: Peso ($)

Main Language: Spanish

Rivers: Grande, Pánuco, Balsas, Grijalva

Area: 758,449 square miles (1,964,375 sq km)

Published by Smart Apple Media
P.O. Box 3263, Mankato, Minnesota 56002

Printed in the United States of America at Corporate Graphics, in North Mankato, Minnesota.

Library of Congress Cataloging-in-Publication Data
Savery, Annabel.
  Mexico / by Annabel Savery.
    p. cm. -- (Been there!)
  Includes index.
  Summary: "Introduces Mexico's major cities and landmarks, such as the Rio Grande, and the Mayan ruins.
Presents the daily activities and ceremonies of the Mexican culture. Includes map diagrams and lessons on
learning to speak and count in Spanish"--Provided by publisher.
  ISBN 978-1-59920-474-1 (library binding)
  1. Mexico--Juvenile literature. I. Title.
  F1208.5.S28 2012
  972--dc22
                    2010039598

Created by Appleseed Editions, Ltd.
Planning and production by Discovery Books Limited
www.discoverybooks.net
Designed by Ian Winton
Edited by Annabel Savery
Map artwork by Stefan Chabluk
Picture research by Tom Humphrey

Picture Credits: Alamy Images: p14 (Bruce Coleman Inc.); Corbis: p5 (Danny Lehman), p7 top (Peter Adams), p8 top (Robert
Holmes), p12 (Diego Giudice), p13 (Alan Copson), p15 (Craig Lovell), pp18-19 (Franz-Marc Frei), p24 (Frans Lemmens), p26
(Danny Lehman), p27 bottom (Keith Dannemiller), p28 bottom (Danny Lehman), p29 (Jeremy Woodhouse/Blend Images);
Galen R Frysinger: p21; Getty Images: p6 (AFP), pp8-9 (Jeremy Woodhouse), pp10-11 (Phil Schermeiseter), p17 (Barcroft
Media), p25 (Maria Stenzel), p27 top (Latin Content); Istockphoto: title page & p22 (tompozzo), p16 (PacoRomero), p23 & p31
(ranplett); Shutterstock: p2 (R Gino Santa Maria), p7 middle (Colman Lerner Gerardo), p28 top (ampFotoStudio); Wikimedia:
p20 (Daniel Schwen).

Cover photos: Istockphoto: right (PacoRomero); Shutterstock: main (Jiri Vatka), left (Ales Liska).

DAD0046
3-2011

987654321

Contents

Off to Mexico!

We are going to Mexico. I am very excited because there is so much to see.

We are going to travel all over the country. The places we are visiting are marked on the map.

UNITED STATES OF AMERICA

Sierra Madre Occidental

Sierra Madre Oriental

Rio Grande

Chihuahua

Los Mochis

Monterrey

Gulf of Mexico

Cancun

Chichen Itza

YUCATAN PENINSULA

Caribbean Sea

Guadalajara

Mexico City

Veracruz

Palenque

BELIZE

Pacific Ocean

MEXICO

GUATEMALA

HONDURAS

0   500 kilometers

0   500 miles

In the center of Mexico is a wide **plateau**, and on either side are long mountain ranges called the *Sierra Madre Oriental* and the *Sierra Madre Occidental*. *Sierra Madre* means "mother range," and *oriental* and *occidental* mean "eastern" and "western."

Here are some things I know about Mexico . . .

- Mexico is in the continent of North America. It is a large country, about three times the size of Texas.

- People wear *sombreros* (right) as part of the national costume. These are big hats with a wide brim to keep off the sun.

- Mexican food is often spicy. Mexican dishes are popular in many countries around the world.

On our trip, I'm going to find out lots more!

Arriving in Mexico City

We fly into the Mexico City airport in the afternoon. After we land, we go straight to the hotel in a taxi.

All the taxis look the same. They are all green and white. And they're the same make of car, too.

It takes a long time to travel through the traffic in the city. It is smelly with exhaust fumes. Mexico City is very **polluted**.

Our driver is very friendly and points out special sites as we pass them.

There is a mix of old and new buildings, such as tall new hotels and old churches.

Mexico City is the most populous in the world. This means it has more people than any other city. More than 19 million people live here.

Exploring the Capital

The next morning, we go into the city center for breakfast. I have *huevos rancheros*. This is a popular dish in Mexico. My plate has *tortillas* with fried eggs on top and tasty *salsa*.

Tortillas are made of corn flour and are round like pancakes, but they are very thin. They are a common food in Mexico and are eaten in many different ways.

After breakfast, we go to the main square in the center of the city. This is called the *Zocalo*. Around the square are big buildings, and in the middle is a huge Mexican flag.

In the city, there are big, colorful bullfighting posters. Bullfighting is an old sport that was brought to Mexico by Spanish people.

The Copper Canyon

Today we are at the west coast port of Los Mochis. From here we will take the train to Chihuahua. On the way, we pass through the Copper Canyon. This is part of the Sierra Madre Occidental.

The canyons were made a long time ago by volcanoes. Over time, the sides have been worn away by rivers and rain. Now there are lots of green plants growing on the rocks.

From the train, we can see deep into the valley. The journey takes 14 hours. On the way, we travel through 86 tunnels and over 37 bridges!

Finally we arrive in the city of Chihuahua. This is the capital of the state of Chihuahua, which is the biggest state in Mexico.

Mountainous Monterrey

From Chihuahua we fly southeast to Monterrey. This is the third largest city in Mexico and the capital of the state of Nuevo Léon. All around the city are the mountains of the Sierra Madre Oriental.

Monterrey is near the border with the United States. Lots of people from Mexico cross the border illegally to look for better jobs. They send money home to their families in Mexico.

Mexico and the United States are divided by a big river. This runs a long way along the border, from the state of Chihuahua to the east coast. You can check this on the map on page 4.

In Mexico, the river is called the Rio Bravo, and in the United States, the Rio Grande. "Rio" comes from the Spanish word for river.

South to Veracruz

From Monterrey we travel south down the coast to Veracruz. This is a state on the east coast of Mexico. It is between the mountains and the sea.

The climate here is warm and tropical. Bananas and other foods grow well here. Some foods are grown to be sold in Mexico. Others are **exported**. Selling food to other countries helps to bring money into Mexico.

Each year there are festivals in Mexico. On the train, a lady tells us that one of the biggest is the *Día de los Muertos*, or "Day of the Dead," held on November 2.

On this day, people remember those who have died by dressing up and making special foods. They visit relatives' graves and set up altars for them. They decorate these with photos and favorite foods.

The Yucatan Peninsula

From Veracruz we fly to the Yucatan **Peninsula**. This is a large piece of land that stretches out into the sea.

A long time ago, people called the Maya had a great civilization in Central America. Some people living in Mexico today are their descendants. The Maya lived mainly on the Yucatan Peninsula. I took this photo of a girl dressed in traditional Mayan clothes.

To the north of the peninsula is the Gulf of Mexico. To the east is the Caribbean Sea.

The land of the Yucatan Peninsula doesn't stop at the coast. It continues under water like a big shelf. As the water is shallow here, it is warm. This makes it a good home for sea creatures such as lobsters, crabs, and fish.

Two Cancuns

Cancun is a big city on the eastern tip of the Yucatan Peninsula. There are two main parts: *Ciudad Cancun* and *Isla Cancun*. We are staying at Isla Cancun.

Isla Cancun is a thin strip of land around a big lagoon.

The beach is long, with white sand and blue sea. I can see why lots of people want to come here. It is very beautiful. But with so many people, it is very crowded.

Until about 50 years ago, Isla Cancun was home to just a few fishermen and their families. Then the government decided to turn it into a **resort**. Many hotels were built for tourists to stay in.

All the people building the hotels lived in a small town. This town grew and grew to become the big city of Ciudad Cancun.

Ancient Ruins

Today we are going to see some of the ancient buildings that the Maya built. The site is called *Chichen Itza*, and it is very famous. We rent a car and drive there from Cancun.

El Castillo

Chichen Itza was a great city of the Mayan people. The biggest building is the *El Castillo* pyramid. There are lots of steep steps up each side. The square part on the top is a temple.

Some of these buildings were built 1,500 years ago, and different groups of people have added to them over the centuries. **Archaeologists** study these buildings to find out about these ancient civilizations.

Although Mayan people still live on the Yucatan Peninsula today, many are leaving their traditional farming jobs to look for work in the cities.

In the Rain Forest

We leave the Yucatan Peninsula and drive south to the city of Palenque. This is another Mayan city. It is in the south of Mexico in the state of Chiapas.

In the city of Palenque, we look at the ruins. There are 500 buildings here, but some have not been uncovered for people to look at.

There are many **indigenous** groups living in Chiapas. Most are related to the Mayan people. Different groups speak different languages, but most people understand Spanish, too.

The ancient city is in the Palenque National Park. The park also contains the *Selva Lacandona*, or Lacandon rain forest. Wild animals such as monkeys, red macaws, toucans, and jaguars live here.

Farming in Mexico

From Palenque we have a long car ride to Guadalajara. This part of the trip will take us through lots of countryside.

We will stop at small towns along the way. Here, people wear clothes made from traditional cloth that is made in the region.

Only a quarter of Mexican people live in the country. Most people live in **urban** areas.

As we travel, we see crops growing and people farming. Some people grow food just to feed themselves and their families. This is called **subsistence** farming.

Other farms are bigger, and crops are grown to sell to people at markets and in shops. These big farms are called *ejidos*.

Maize

The main crop grown in Mexico is maize. Maize flour (or corn flour) is used to make the tortillas that people eat with most meals.

In Guadalajara City

Guadalajara is the second largest city in Mexico. The city is warm, and there are lots of people shopping and talking with friends.

After being in the country, it is strange being in the city again. Here, many people wear western clothes, such as jeans and T-shirts.

Lots of people in Guadalajara are wearing soccer shirts. *Fútbol*, or soccer, is the most popular sport in Mexico. Guadalajara is in the first division of the Mexican soccer league.

Children in Mexico have to go to school from the ages of 6 to 14. Different age groups have lessons at different times. Some children start early in the morning and finish at lunchtime. Others start after lunch and go on until the early evening.

Spanish Settlers

Exploring Guadalajara is hungry work, so we buy *tacos* from a street stall. These are crunchy tortillas that are folded around beans, cheese, and spicy tomato salsa. Yum!

Next, we go to the cathedral. This was built by Spanish people who came to Mexico more than 500 years ago. They brought the Roman Catholic religion with them.

While we are having dinner, a group of mariachis walk past playing instruments and singing. Mariachis are musicians who play traditional Mexican music.

The mariachis are wearing traditional costumes. They have big, wide sombreros on.

We leave Guadalajara in the morning and go back to Mexico City on the train. From here we are going to fly home. I can't wait to tell all my friends about our trip to Mexico!

My First Words in Spanish

Many languages are spoken in Mexico. The most common and official language is Spanish. Mexican Spanish has words from old indigenous languages mixed in, too.

Buenos dias
(*say* **Bway-nohs dee-ahs**)   Hello

Adios (*say* **Ah-dee-ohs**)   Goodbye

Como estás?
(*say* **Koh-moh ay-stahs**)   How are you?

Como te llamas?
(*say* **Koh-moh tay yah-mahs**)   What is your name?

Me llamo Alice.
(*say* **May yah-moh Alice**)   My name is Alice.

Counting 1 to 10

1 **uno** (*say* **oo-noh**)

2 **dos** (*say* **dohs**)

3 **tres** (*say* **trays**)

4 **cuatro** (*say* **kwat-roh**)

5 **cinco** (*say* **sink-o**)

6 **seis** (*say* **says**)

7 **siete** (*say* **see-ay-tay**)

8 **ocho** (*say* **oh-cho**)

9 **nueve** (*say* **new-ay-vay**)

10 **diez** (*say* **dee-ays**)

Words to Remember

altar a raised table or platform used for religious ceremonies

archaeologist a scientist who learns about the past by digging up old objects and buildings and examining them

civilization a large group of people who live in an organized society with their own laws, arts, and customs

descendants people who are the family of people who lived a long time ago

ejidos commercial farms

export to sell goods to another country

illegally against the law

indigenous people who originally come from a place

peninsula a strip of land that is almost completely surrounded by water

plateau an area of high, flat land

polluted made dirty or harmful by mixing with dangerous substances

populous full of people

resort a place where people go to relax and have fun while on vacation

subsistence a type of farming in which the farmer grows just enough to feed his or her family

urban built-up areas, such as cities and towns

Index

Learning More about Mexico

Books

Looking at Mexico (Looking at Countries) Kathleen Pohl, Gareth Stevens, 2008.
Mexico (A Visit to) Rob Alcraft, Heinemann Library, 2008.
Welcome to Mexico (Welcome to the World) Mary Berendes, Child's World, 2007.
We Visit Mexico (Your Land and My Land) Tammy Gagne, Mitchell Lane, 2010.

Web Sites

Geography for Kids, Geography Online, and Geography Games
   http://www.kidsgeo.com/index.php
National Geographic Kids, People & Places
   http://kids.nationalgeographic.com/kids/places/find/mexico
SuperKids Geography directory, lots of sites to help with geography learning.
   http://www.super-kids.com/geography.html